Published by Damaso & Valeria Publishing
damasosaka.com

TABLE OF CONTENTS PAGE

INTRODUCTION

This story is about Luz and her six years old daughter Valeria. Valeria is starting to learn that with money, she can buy lots of toys and candy. The family has a dog named Betty. She loves treats as much as Valeria loves candy.

Luz understands that Valeria is young, and her dream to earn money to buy lots of toys and candy is a good start. She also understands that her daughter's future is dependent on the values that she teaches her at an early age. She knows that teaching her about money and the value of a penny will help her understand the importance of a budget that will lead to financial planning and success.

my Betty
My
Bank accounts
my money
my accounts
my savings
Valeria
Me and my mom Luz
$1
QUARTERS
DIMES
NICKELS
PENNY

Hmmm... why is the penny jar empty?
My
accounts
my accounts
my savings
Valeria
Me and my mom Luz
DIMES
NICKELS
PENNY

Valeria, why are you throwing away your money?
PENNY
QUARTERS

It is not money, mommy.
It is a penny. I save the quarters.
Why do you think that pennies are not money?
Because I wanted to buy candy in my school and Ms. Angy told me that I needed $1.
QUARTERS

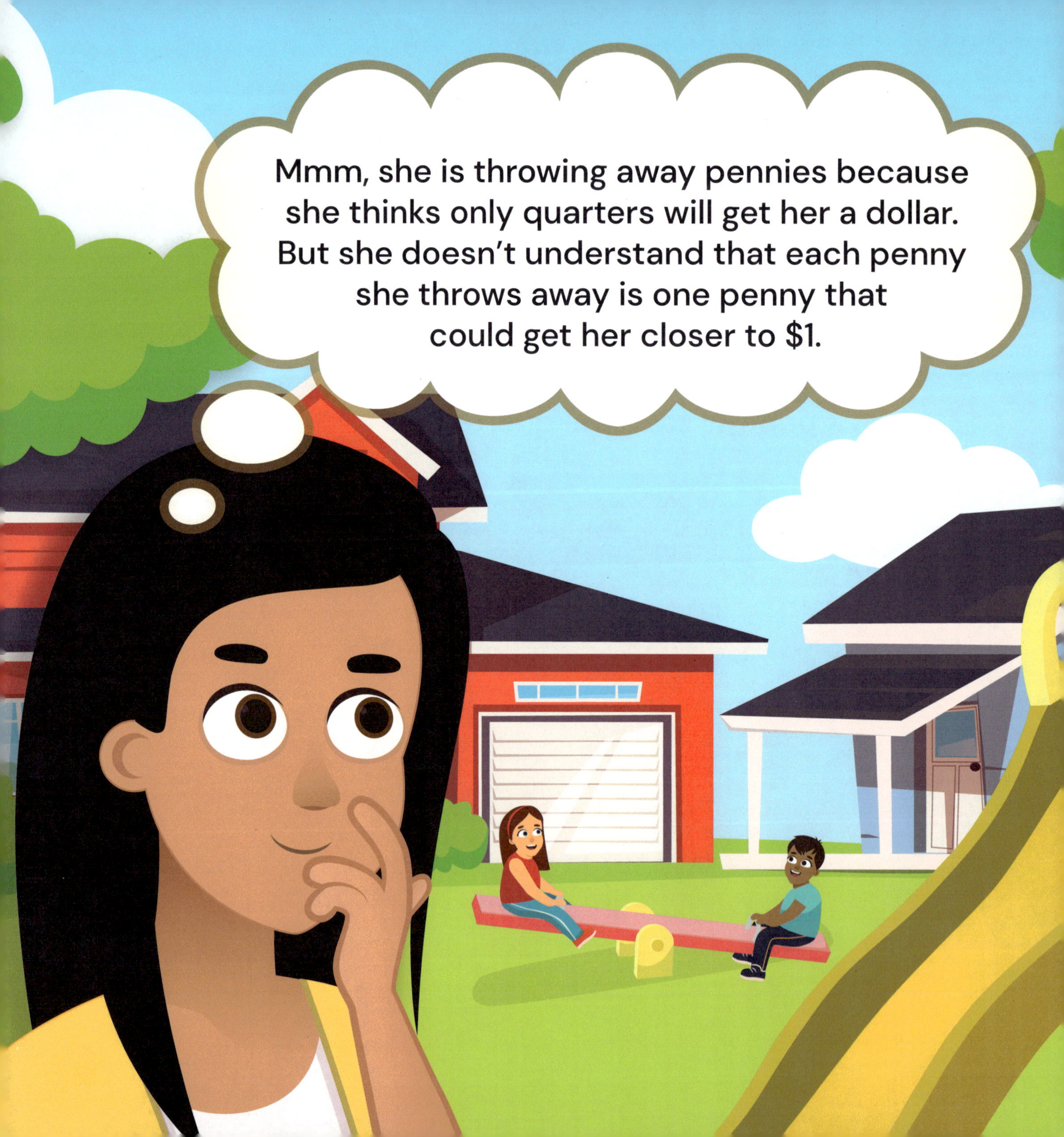
Mmm, she is throwing away pennies because she thinks only quarters will get her a dollar. But she doesn't understand that each penny she throws away is one penny that could get her closer to $1.

I need to teach her the value in a penny. I will use her block tower game.
Let's go home!

Would you like to play your favorite game?
Block tower! Yes, yes, mama, building blocks!

my Betty
My Bank accounts
my money
my accounts
my savings
Valeria
Me and my mom Luz
$1
QUARTERS
DIMES
NICKELS
PENNY
Woof!
Valeria, can we play, can we play?
Woof!

Now that we have built the block tower, go ahead, and remove the first block.

What just happened to
your tower?
The building fell, mommy!

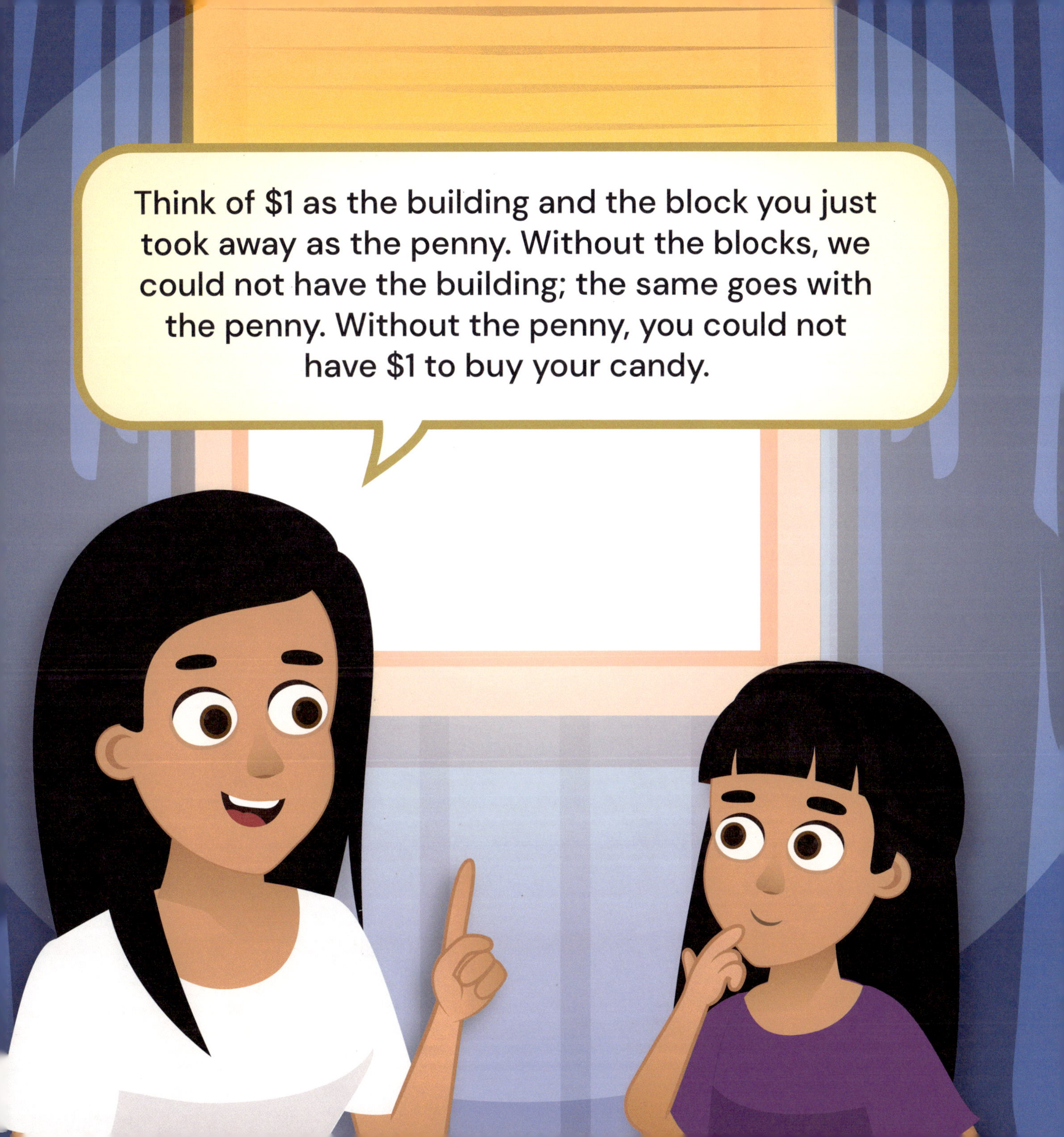
Think of $1 as the building and the block you just took away as the penny. Without the blocks, we could not have the building; the same goes with the penny. Without the penny, you could not have $1 to buy your candy.

100
PENNIES
=
$1
+
=
my accounts
my savings
Valeria
Me and my mom Luz
DIMES
NICKELS
PENNY

If you have $1 and you throw away one penny you no longer have $1; you see why pennies are so important?
Now I get it. I never thought about it that way.
TERS
DIMES
NICKEL

You don't have to stop saving when you get to a dollar. You can save as many pennies as you want!
Yes, mommy, I will save all my pennies.
PENNY

Now that you have saved your pennies, we are going to the bank to see how much money you have saved.
Bank accounts
my money
my accounts
my savings
Valeria
PENNY

PART 2: BUDGET AND SAVING

THE PENNY BANK

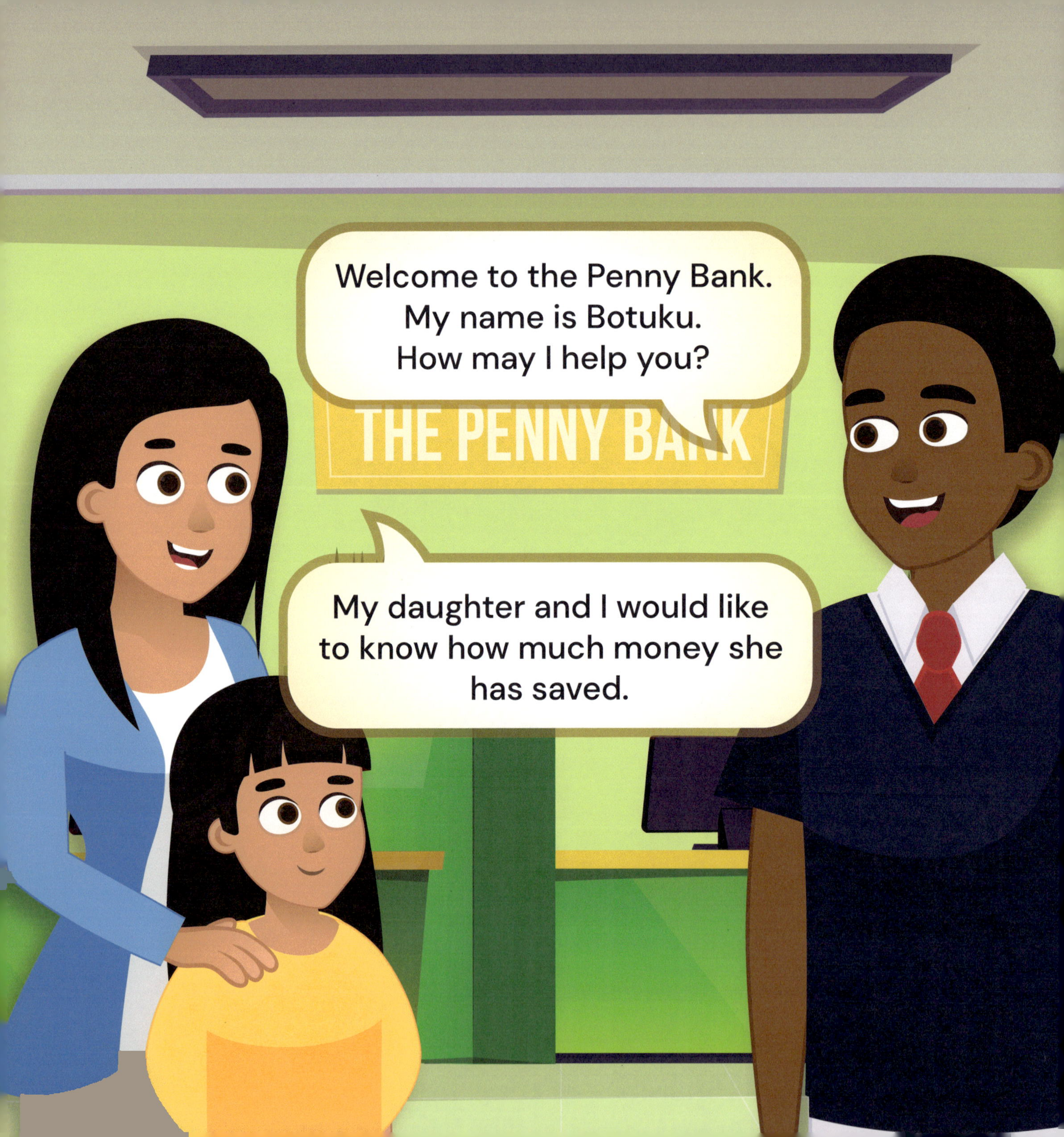
Welcome to the Penny Bank. My name is Botuku. How may I help you?
THE PENNY BANK
My daughter and I would like to know how much money she has saved.

What is your name?
My name is Valeria.
Hi Valeria, nice to meet you. Let us see how much money you have saved.

Congratulations, you were able to save $10.
$10!

Great job! You saved $10 by saving lots of pennies.
THE PENN
Now, I want you to save more pennies, nickels, dimes, quarters, and dollars. Once you save $30, come back to the bank to open a savings account.

$1
QUARTERS
DIMES
NICKELS
PENNY
I have a bank account at home.

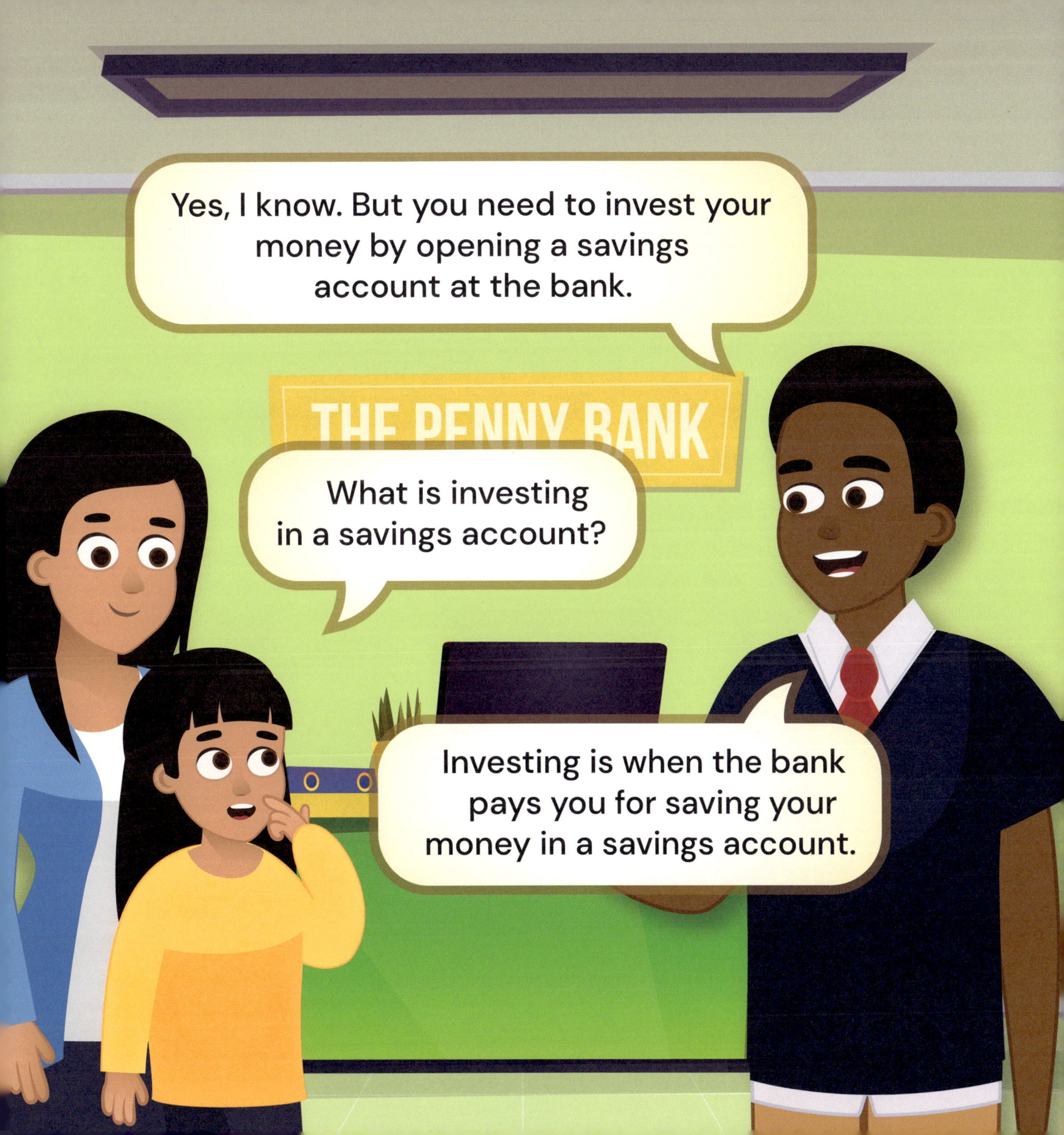
Yes, I know. But you need to invest your money by opening a savings account at the bank.
THE PENNY BANK
What is investing in a savings account?
Investing is when the bank pays you for saving your money in a savings account.

A vault is a large safe in which banks store money.

So you will pay me to save my money? Wow!
Yes, we will pay you to save your money at the bank.

10
10

Yes?
Mama, mama!

I will never throw my pennies away again. I will always keep my pennies!
Why did you change your mind?

Because it is money, a lot of money, I got $10 from my pennies.
Well said, my daughter. Every penny counts in your bank account.
10
10

She is finally getting it!
If pennies can get me $10, then I will keep saving to get a lot more money.

Budget: $35
Toy: $5
Bank
$30
What does that mean, "budget"?
nd my mom Luz
ARTERS
DIMES
NICKE

A budget is planning what to do with your money.
Just like we are doing right now:
- $5 is for your toy and
- $30 is to invest into your first bank account.
Toy: $5
Bank account: $30
Me and my mom Luz
DIMES
NICKELS

You have now saved $35. Good job. I am very proud of you!
Budget: $35
Toy: $5
Bank account: $30
Me and my mom Luz
RTERS
DIMES
NICKEL

$5

Best Toys

THE PENNY BANK

Congratulations, Valeria, you have just opened your first bank account.
THE PENNY BANK
Bank account

E PENNY BANK
Mommy, I bought my toy, and I opened my first bank account.
Bank account

You have achieved so much!
✓ You budgeted for planning what to do with your money.
✓ By budgeting, you were able to save.
✓ By saving, you were able to buy your toy and invest into your first bank account.
You make me so proud.

INDEX

The following concepts are important, because they build the foundation of your child's financial vocabulary, understanding, and planning.

FINANCIAL PLANNING:

Your short, middle, and long terms money goals

Example: I want to buy a toy.

- how much is the toy? $10
- how much money do I have now? $4
- how much more money do I need to buy the toy? $6
- what steps do I have to take to get $6?

Money: It is an instrument in the economy that allows you to buy goods and services.

Buy: Action of getting something in exchange for money.

Budget: You need a budget to plan.

- By planning, you can save money to buy your toy.

Success: To be able to enjoy what you have.

Bank Account: The place where you save your money. investing/investment [from a savings point of view].

Savings Account: Saving money for future needs.

LETTER TO PARENTS

The value in a penny

Take a penny out of a hundred-dollar bill, and you no longer have a hundred-dollar bill; rather, you now have ninety-nine dollars and ninety-nine cents. This is how fundamental the penny is. $100 - $.01 = $99.99

The value in a penny is a secret that has been uncovered by those who live in abundance and can transfer their wealth to future generations. Remember, if the pennies are not going into your bank account, they are going into someone else's bank account. The pennies in this concept could be understood as membership subscriptions, impulsive buying, high-interest rate borrowing, credit cards, student loans, and much more that drain your ability to live a stable lifestyle.

DEDICATIONS

Thanks, Luz Amparo and Allan Guerra; you're an inspiration - your daughter

By: Damaso Saka

Co-Writer & Editor: Valeria Inagan

Illustrators: Alina Kutnyaya, Yevhenii Kupriienko

Made in the USA
Monee, IL
05 November 2026

67379949R00031